Decrease

Todd Galberth

Published in Greenville, SC by:
Stella's Boy Music

Cover Design: Rickey Craig
Layout Design: Erica Smith

Book Project Management:
Start Write, Inc.

ISBN 10: 0-9984271-2-8
ISBN 13: 978-0-9984271-2-6

Contents

Introduction

About four years ago, as I was preparing to teach a workshop, I asked God a question to which I thought I knew the answer. I knew what I had read and studied in the past, but I sincerely wanted to know what His definition of worship is. Feeling as though I already knew the answer, I really didn't think that I would get a response, or at least not a speedy one. However, as soon as I asked the question, these words flowed out of my spirit: "Worship is my heartfelt attitude toward my Creator, which causes me to live my life with Christ as the center and object of my affection, One Whom I honor daily with my life." It was liberating! The part that I couldn't shake was "Whom I honor daily with my life."

We have boxed worship into an event — an event in which we partake once or twice a week at our local assemblies. We've made worship something that we do, a scheduled ritual. The reality is that we spend more time outside of church than we do in it. Therefore, we have a greater opportunity and responsibility to glorify our Father outside of the four walls of church rather than inside them. You are missing out on an amazing opportunity to worship God through your daily life if you're waiting for Sunday to roll around again and again. Your worship platform isn't a stage or church service; it's on your job, in your home, the grocery store, parking lots, and through your relationships with others. That's how He gets glory—through your serving, compassion, love, respect, and charity. That's worship! The act of worship means very little if you don't maintain a lifestyle of worship.

The next 21 days have very little to do with the "act" of worship, but EVERYTHING to do with the life of a worshipper. Decrease is a 21-day journey mapped out to draw you closer to God and really allow Him to be glorified in your everyday life. No more rituals! It's about a relationship—a walk with God.

"Lord, I decrease so that You can increase; have Your way through me. Don't let my will get in the way. Don't let my flesh drive You away. Lord, I decrease; have Your way through me." This entire devotional is based on a song/prayer I wrote. It's a prayer that I pray before I minister, and a prayer I challenge you to pray daily. Don't allow your ideas of how you think things should go to cloud your heart and spirit. Jesus said it best in the garden of Gethsemane, "…not my will but your will be done." Let's spend the next 21 days and beyond posturing our lives upon this prayer. Are you ready? Here we go! It's time to decrease!

Day 1: Lord?

[8] If we live, we live for the Lord; and if we die, we die for the Lord. So, whether we live or die, we belong to the Lord. [9] For this very reason, Christ died and returned to life so that he might be the Lord of both the dead and the living (Romans 14:8-9).

I struggled with starting here on the first day of this journey. I didn't know if I wanted to start so heavy on the first day, but if we don't establish Him as Lord over our lives, the next 21 days won't mean much. I think most people know what it means for Jesus to be their Savior, but when it comes to His being their Lord, many don't have a true understanding of what that means. Jesus made the decision to become our Savior. We had no hand in that decision at all; however, the choice of His being our Lord is totally ours. We must choose Him and submit to His Lordship.

We are a part of HIS kingdom and rule; consequently, we must bring our hearts, will, and life UNDER His headship. That's when "no longer my will, but thy will be done" becomes a reality. Let's start day one off with simply submitting ourselves to His rule and reign over our lives. That's definitely easier said than done, but trust me, it's so worth it! When you allow Him to be Lord over your life, it also makes Him responsible for your life.

On the flip side, when you make the decision to be in control of yourself, you become the master of your fate. What does that mean? The responsibility for your life falls solely on you. Maybe it's just me, but I would rather have the God Who created the Heavens and the Earth and who knows the beginning from the end to be in complete control over my life. The reality is that we all have a headship to which we've submitted. The question is: whose headship to whom will you continue to submit?

PRAY THIS WITH ME:

Father, I'm so grateful to call You my savior, but I also thank You for being my Lord. I submit my life to You. I give You permission to be my Lord! I place all that I am and all that I have under your Lordship. Order my steps, Lord. Lead and guide me. No longer will I just bring You my plans and goals, but I humbly ask what it is that you require of me... and, whatever that is, my answer will be "Yes, Lord."

Medicine Music:

"I Surrender"— Hillsong

Day 2: 2nd Place

Do not worship any other god, for the LORD, whose name is Jealous, is a jealous God (Ex. 34:14).

In order for our lives to be under His Lordship, it is vital that we let Him take His rightful place. He can't just "fit" around what we do; He has to be the "center" of our everyday lives. As humans, we honor what we value. We put our time, energy and resources things that we value, especially our money. Our treasure is where our heart is. Where does God fit into your value system? How important is He outside of your Sunday morning experience? He should be more than your "Sunday morning Jesus." He desires relationship, not religion. If we box Him into a day of the week, He's no more important than a yoga class or a weekly visit to the grocery store. His heart yearns to be our first love, not an afterthought or merely something to do when convenient. He wants to be God in our lives every day rather than our fair-weather God on Whom we call on our bad day, sick day, or broke day. If He's only a priority when we need Him, we reduce Him to a good luck charm. Don't miss out on a relationship with Him that would allow you not only to call Him Father but also FRIEND.

PRAY THIS WITH ME:

Father, I thank You for being my savior and my Lord, but I also thank You for being my friend. Thank You for being faithful and consistent. Forgive me for not putting You where You rightfully belong in my life. Today, I make a decision to put You at the center of my life. Today, I make You priority.

Medicine Music:
"One Thing"— House Fires

Day 3: Relationship Goals

Here I am! I stand at the door and knock. If anyone hears my voice and opens the door, I will come in and eat with that person, and they with me (Rev. 3:20).

If your view of the Father is His sitting on a huge golden throne looking down at us and ruling only from a place of authority, you're so wrong. Remember: He wants relationship! As a child, I remember the deacons praying in our opening prayer, "He sits high, and He looks low." Though it sounds good, He would much rather walk with us than rule with an iron fist over us. This character trait is what I love about Him so much. He actually desires a relationship...a relationship with me. Wow! It can be somewhat easy to view Him as Father, Savior, or maybe even Lord, but I can see how "friend" can feel a little weird. However, that's what makes Christianity so special.

He's not this God who just longs to be worshipped. He also longs for a bond that cannot be broken with us. I love how John penned it, "I'm no longer calling you servants because servants don't understand what their master is thinking and planning. No, I've named you friends because I've let you in on everything I've heard from the Father" (John 15:15). You're not on the outside looking in. You're His friend. So what makes a friendship/relationship great? Communication! Let's start here today. Let's communicate with Him. Prayer is a two-way street. Talk and listen. Tell Him how you feel before you bring your issue to some human who may not have the answers you need. Tell Him what He means to you. Talk to Him! He wants to hear from you Every day, in good times and bad. Hey, that's what friends are for.

This is where I would normally say, "Pray this with me," but today I want you to take a minute or so to just thank Him for being your friend. Go!

Medicine Music:
"First Loved Me"— Covenant Worship

Day 4: Relationship Goals Part II

…"Truly I tell you, whatever you did for one of the least of these brothers and sisters of mine, you did for me" (Matt. 25:40).

Yesterday, we wanted to establish how important relationship is to our Father. Today, I need you to see how relationships with each other are just as important. John put it like this, "If anyone boasts, 'I love God,' and goes right on hating his brother or sister, thinking nothing of it, he is a liar. If he won't love the person he can see, how can he love the God he can't see?" (I John 4:20). All of our energy can't just go into our vertical relationship with God. We have to put the same energy into our horizontal relationships with people. That's worship, too! God is glorified when we love and respect each other. Even Jesus said that the second GREATEST commandment is to "love your neighbor as yourself." That's a big statement! There are a lot of religious people who seemingly have incredible relationships with God, but treat people horribly. Get this: most of us go to church once or twice a week for about 1-2 hours per service. That would be an average of 4 hours a week or 16 hours a month. There are 672 hours in a month. Do the math: 672-16=656 hours. We spend the majority of our time outside of the four walls of the church with people—our family, friends, coworkers, and strangers.

What do these relationships look like? I want my relationship with God to spill over into my relationships with others.

Pray This With Me:

Father, I thank You for loving me and wanting to have a relationship with someone like me. Help me to treat my family, friends, and strangers the way I would treat myself. Forgive me for being selfish. Give me a passion to love people. I want to be Your light in this dark world.

Medicine Music:
"Christ Representers"—
Jonathan McReynolds

Day 5: Get "I" Out of the Way

But seek ye first his kingdom and his righteousness, and all these things will be given to you as well (Matt. 6:33).

Some of you have a sincere desire to be used by God. You know exactly what you want to do for Him. That's great, but when was the last time you asked him what He wanted from you? Normally, we bring him OUR plans and OUR goals but rarely do we posture ourselves to really seek His will for our lives. It's easier to bring Him our ideas and thoughts rather than put the energy into seeking His plan/will for our life. I've been there. I knew what I wanted to do, where I wanted to do it, and when I wanted to do it — and He said, "Nope!"

I thought those things were what He wanted, but when I became truly honest with myself, it was what I wanted to do. I didn't find true fulfillment until I surrendered my will and said, "My answer is 'Yes' to whatever You want. I don't care how it looks or where it is, 'yes Lord.'" Sometimes it won't look like what you originally planned, but you will experience the thing that most people would give their right arm for — fulfillment. People will work tirelessly for years, sacrifice, and try everything under the sun for fulfillment. A new house won't do it. More money may provide pleasure for a season, but it will eventually leave you unfulfilled. True fulfillment comes from being in the will of God. I know this is contrary to our current culture of "do you" and "make your own happiness." That stuff is temporary! Today, I challenge you to wholeheartedly seek His will. I promise that you'll find it/ Him in the seeking. "...seek, and ye shall find; knock, and it shall be opened unto you!" (Matthew 7:7).

PRAY THIS WITH ME:

Lord, I want Your will for my life. For years I've brought my goals and ambitions to You but today, I abandon my plans and seek Your plan for my life. I give You my will for Yours. I don't want a temporary fix anymore. I want to be fulfilled. I want to be in Your will.

Medicine Music:
"Lord, I Decrease"— Todd Galberth

Day 6: Something You've Never Seen

Now to him who is able to do immeasurably more than all we ask or imagine, according to his power that is at work within us, 21to him be glory in the church and in Christ Jesus throughout all generations, for ever and ever! Amen (Eph. 3:20).

What if God wants to move differently than what you expected? What if He wants to move in a unique way? If your mind is made up that things should happen a "particular way," you might miss an amazing opportunity for God to give you a "one-of-a-kind miracle," or use you in a powerful and unique way! We often look at how God is moving in someone else's life and make the mistake of becoming jealous and coveting what he or she has. Listen, I know it's been said a million times, but "What God has for you is for you." The problem is that you can't get what's yours while lusting over what God is doing in someone else's life. Don't box Him into your latest experience. I feel strongly that this year will be filled with unique opportunities, blessings, and miracles for those who take God out of their religious boxes. Every miracle Jesus did was unique! Who else was spitting on the ground, making mud, and putting it on blind men's eyes? That was a one of a kind miracle!

Our problem is that we can't see past what we've already seen. There was a man in John 5 who was waiting at the pool of Bethesda for years. He was trying to receive his healing the same way everyone else did. Then Jesus came by, asked him one question and told him to take up his bed and walk! The man thought that his miracle would happen like those who came before him but Jesus wanted to give him a different experience. Likewise, He wants to give you something different. The question is: are you ready to see something you've never seen?

PRAY THIS WITH ME:

Lord, forgive me for placing You in a box. Open the eyes of my heart to see You through an entirely different lens. I'm not holding You to my last experience anymore. Blow my mind! I thank You that I'm getting ready to see something I've never seen!

Medicine Music:
"I'm Getting Ready"— Tasha Cobbs Leonard

Day 7: Use Me

Each of you should use whatever gift you have received to serve others, as faithful stewards of God's grace in its various forms (I Pet. 4:10).

When I was 16 years old I gave my life to the Lord. After I asked Him to save me, there was one more thing I wanted Him to do. And that was to use me for His glory. I didn't know anything about recording a CD, leading worship at mega churches or traveling around the world to sing. All I wanted was to simply to be used by God. I'm sure many of you who are reading this have a sincere desire to be used by God, but if you think that's going to happen within the confines of the building called "church," you are sadly mistaken. I mentioned earlier, God will get more glory out of your life outside of church than inside of the four walls. We have an amazing opportunity every day to keep our eyes and hearts open to be used by the Father. One of the prayers I pray consistently is "Lord make me someone's miracle today." I want to be the answer to someone's problem. That desire came with age and maturity. When I was a child, I looked forward to receiving gifts on Christmas. Now, as an adult, I get more joy out of being the gift giver.

It is very easy to be consumed by our own issues and problems. We've all been there. Sometimes, life just happens, and we get caught up in our own world to the point where we lose our desire to be a blessing to someone else. There is such an unexplainable joy that comes from helping people. I'm speaking of acts of service that aren't captured on your cell phones and posted on our social media. I think this generation has totally lost sight of the fact that what you do secretly, God will reward openly.

What God is going to do in the Earth is going to be done through people—through me, and through you. The Bible says that the harvest is plentiful, but the laborers are few. We have to change our mindset from just wanting a blessing to being a blessing. God wants to use you, and it may not be on a stage or platform.

Pray This With Me:

Father, make me a blessing. Today, I want to be someone's miracle. I put my problems to the side, and I ask You to use me. If it's a kind word, my resources, or praying for someone, I want You to use me!

Medicine Music:
"I'm Yours"— Casey J

Day 8: Directions

I will instruct you and teach you in the way you should go; I will counsel you with my loving eye on you (Ps. 32:8).

I went to the bathroom at a very well-known restaurant to wash my hands. The paper towel dispenser read, "Place hands under dispenser to activate." What I wanted/needed was directly in front of me, but I couldn't "activate" it until I followed the directions. How close are you to the thing you've prayed for? Maybe you can't obtain it because you haven't followed the directions. Accordingly, if I waved my hands in front of or above the dispenser, the paper towel would not have dispensed. I know you're doing "some"thing, but are you doing the "right thing?"

It's frustrating when you put your time and energy into something and see no results. I'm sure that's how Peter felt after fishing all night and catching nothing. Then Jesus showed up and told them, "I know you're tired and disappointed, but go back out and follow these directions—throw your net on the other side!" The blessing they received from following his directions was too big for them. They had to call other boats to come help them reap the harvest. That's what happens when you follow directions. You see fruit. They did exactly what He said. Partial obedience is complete disobedience. He has given us instructions, a road map to success. It's all in His WORD. No matter what you face, there's a scripture, chapter, and book for it!

I know sometimes doing things the right way can seem a little tough when you're watching other people take short-cuts, but if you take shortcuts to get it, you'll have to continue to take shortcuts to keep it! Doing it His way is not only right; it's better!

PRAY THIS WITH ME:

God, I thank You for Your Word. Your Word heals me, frees me, saves me, directs me. Forgive me for not following Your directions. Holy Spirit, help me. Help me not to lean to my own understanding or choose my own way. I want to follow Your directions, Lord. I submit my will to Yours, and I will trust Your Word.

Medicine Music:
"Lead Me"— KJ Scriven

Day 9: Worshipping in the Rain

Give thanks in all circumstances; for this is God's will for you in Christ Jesus (I Thess. 5:18).

Nothing is more disheartening than feeling as if things are finally coming together and that you're moving forward, only to be knocked backward by life. I know this feeling all too well. It's deflating. Depression attempts to set in, and you lose your drive to accomplish the smallest of tasks. You can't believe it's "raining" again!

Now, two things can happen: you can succumb to the pressure of the storm or stand on God's Word and keep moving forward. Doing nothing will never help you. When you don't know what to do, do the things you know to do. Take the scriptures you know, sermons you've heard, encouragement you've been given, and work it. God will never put more on you than you can bear. If He allowed it, He equipped you to go through it and to overcome it. Sometimes, God won't pull you out of the rain; He'll just give you an umbrella. Sometimes, the rain is necessary, and if you get pulled out prematurely, you won't learn the lesson the "downpour" was designed to teach.

Take a deep breath, worship through this, love through this, and encourage others while you are in it! Keep serving. Weeping may endure for a night, but joy comes in the morning! Embrace the storm, and learn from it. God doesn't waste anything! It may hurt now, but it's working for your good. Stay under the umbrella of His Word, and keep worshipping in the rain.

PRAY THIS WITH ME:

Lord, thank You for counting me worthy to suffer for the Kingdom. Forgive me for focusing on my situation rather than You. I acknowledge that You're sovereign and that You're building character in me. I trust You and Your plan for me. I thank You for choosing me to bring glory to You.

Medicine Music:
"You Hold My World"—
Israel Houghton

Day 10:
The Inconvenience of Convenience

²Consider it pure joy, my brothers, and sisters, whenever you face trials of many kinds, ³ because you know that the testing of your faith produces perseverance. ⁴ Let perseverance finish its work so that you may be mature and complete, not lacking anything (James 1:2-4).

The definition of convenience is the "state of being able to proceed with something with little effort or difficulty." Be honest; we love convenience and comfort. We love being in a position to put in the least amount of effort and get optimal results. I've learned in my walk with the Lord that very little has been produced in my life from a comfortable place. In fact, King David wrote one of his most famous Psalms from an amazing place in his life: "I will bless the LORD at all times; his praise shall continually be in my mouth." This memorable song wasn't written in the midst of a great victory. It was composed from a place of inconvenience, on the run for his life. You will be surprised at what God can do for you and through you from an inconvenient state. Some things cannot be adequately produced from a comfortable place. Some of the greatest songs, messages, and testimonies have come from people whom God pushed out of their comfort zones.

Are you too comfortable? When is the last time you've been pushed or you've pushed yourself toward greatness? Greatness is in you, but it's not going to happen by osmosis. If it's going to happen, it will be because you had the courage to step out of your comfortable/convenient place and make moves. Work as if it depends on you, and pray as though it depends on God. You're not average. There's greatness in you because the Great one lives in you!

Pray This With Me:

Lord, I realize that there's greatness in me. I have seen my states of inconvenience as challenges rather than opportunities for You to take me to the next level of destiny in You. I embrace the inconveniences, cast down fear and anticipate what You will do through me as I step out of my comfort zone. Thank You for grace.

Medicine Music:
"I Want To Be Used By You"—
Deluge Band

Day 11:
The Proactive Life

In their hearts, humans plan their course, but the LORD determines our steps (Prov. 16:9).

"You're a day late and a dollar short!" I used to hear older people say that a lot when I was a kid. It's the feeling of being one step behind — almost, but no. The reason that we find ourselves behind and never quite hitting the mark is that we stay in a reactive posture. If you're always reacting to things, situations, and all that life is constantly throwing at you, you're always going to be playing catch up. Instead of waiting for something to happen, find yourself being proactive. PREPARATION is the key. Prepare now, study now, learn now, PRAY NOW! You're going to miss opportunities or not be ready when life throws you a curve ball if you're consistently reacting.

I found myself there this week. I had something to come my way that I didn't expect, and I found myself praying more and going into the Word deeper...reacting! I should have already been in that place. It's very easy to slip into a relaxed place in our lives when things are going well, forgetting that we have an adversary who is consistently seeking whom he may devour.

We can't just go to God when we're in trouble. He has to be the center of our everyday lives, the Object of our affection; the one Whom we communicate with DAILY. Let's get on the offensive in every area of our lives!

Let's Pray:

Lord, keep Your Word always on my lips that I may meditate on it day and night. I want to be careful to do what is written in it. I trust that You will make me prosperous and successful. (Ref. Joshua 1:8).

Medicine Music:
"You Have Me"— Gungor

Day 12: Faith Over Fear

The Spirit you received does not make you slaves so that you live in fear again; rather, the Spirit you received brought about your adoption to sonship. And by him, we cry, "Abba, Father" (Rom. 9:15).

I'll never forget that Sunday I heard my Pastor say, "There is going to come a time in every man's life that he has to make a significant "decision" that is going to propel him into his destiny or deny him from it." I believe that decision for me came a few weeks ago in the form of a question: faith or fear? Nobody could make that decision for me, and nobody will be able to make it for you. You cannot walk on water from inside the boat. It was scary, but I did it. I did something I've never done, and I saw something I've never seen!

It may be in these 21 days or afterward, but your "day" is coming, and you'll have to make a decision that will affect your destiny. Fear cannot be the reason why you don't make that decision. I know about fear and anxiety all too well. It relentlessly grips your mind and emotions. It can make you physically sick. Even when nothing has happened, it creeps in. Anxiety is a down payment on something that may NEVER happen. Fear is not a physical battle; it's a spiritual battle. Fear is not from God! "God has not given us the spirit of fear, but of power, and of love, and of a sound mind" (2 Timothy 1:7). Fear is a spirit, and you have the authority over it.

Refuse to let fear sway your decisions or stop you from making them. Meditate on God's word. If you know how to worry, you know how to meditate. Make a faith move. Your future depends on it. Your business is depending on it. Your children may be depending on this decision. Let's walk on water. Let's see something we've never seen. Choose FAITH over fear.

PRAY THIS WITH ME:

Father, I rebuke the fear of anxiety. I've allowed it to stagnate my position in the

Kingdom. I stand on Your Word and receive the power, love and sound mind that You've promised me. I declare that I'm no longer controlled by fear. I choose to answer Your call. I choose to trust You. I'm ready to see something I've never seen.

Medicine Music:
"No Longer Slaves"— Bethel Music

Day 13: Keep that Room Clean!

Be very careful, then, how you live—not as unwise but as wise, making the most of every opportunity, because the days are evil (Eph. 5:15-16).

When I was a lad, I hated cleaning my room. When my mom told me to clean it, I would do a horrible job. I would do just enough to be able to say I did it. Clothes would be stuffed in the closet, and I just shoved everything else underneath my bed. I'll never forget her coming into my room and saying, "Todd, it's easier to keep a clean room clean than a dirty one." She was trying to get me to understand that it was a lot easier to maintain something than to start from scratch every time. It's like working out. Once you get into a rhythm, you're good; however, the moment you take a few days off or maybe a few weeks off, you find it extremely hard to start back!

Our walk with the Father can be very similar. We will start becoming disciplined in reading our Word consistently and getting up early to pray and the moment something interrupts our rhythm, we stop. We find ourselves saying, "I'll just start again next week," or "Well, I've been doing so well I can take today off and start tomorrow." A good excuse is still an EXCUSE. You can always find a good excuse to stop. Always. Don't let life, people, or circumstances stop what you've worked so hard to start. Ask yourself every day, "Is it worth it?" Is this excuse worth my losing my momentum and risking the loss of what I've worked so hard to build? Aren't you tired of starting over? It takes too much energy! Again, in the words of Stella, "It's easier to keep a clean room clean than a dirty one." Keep it clean.

PRAY THIS WITH ME:

Father, I am confident that You've begun a good work in me, and I stand on Your word that says that You'll perform it until the day of Jesus Christ. I acknowledge that I'm nothing without You, but with You, I can maintain my confidence and momentum. I put my hope in You. I will do my part to maintain my ways before You by receiving Your guidance and instruction. I want You to be pleased with my life.

Medicine Music:

"Maintain"— Jonathan McReynolds

Day 14: I Choose You

Therefore, I urge you, brothers and sisters, in view of God's mercy, to offer your bodies as a living sacrifice, holy and pleasing to God—this is your true and proper worship (Rom. 12:1).

Jesus showed us by giving His life that we were His number-one priority. He hung, bled, and died to prove to us that there is no length to which He wouldn't go. He willingly gave Himself as a ransom for our sins. The key word is willingly; He wanted to. Paul said, "I beseech you, therefore, brethren by the mercies of God to present your bodies as a living sacrifice." When you present yourself, you come on your own free will. It's very different from surrendering. To surrender means that you have no other choices and that something has forced your hand to give up. When you present yourself, you make a conscious decision to show up. It's what you want to do, not what you're forced to do.

That's the kind of relationship the Father wants, He desires a relationship where you WILLINGLY choose Him, serve Him and honor Him with your everyday life, not because you're in trouble or have no other options, but because you love Him. He wants to be our first love. What do you love more than Him? Who/what has your heart and attention? Make a decision today to choose Him over everything, and then willingly come. Please understand that you don't have to be perfect or "have it all together" to come. He just wants you—the imperfect, jacked up, messed up you!

PRAY THIS WITH ME:

Father, today I renew my commitment to serve You with my whole heart. I repent for putting things and people before You. Today, I say, "Yes" to You and You alone. I choose to seek Your Kingdom first. Your Word says that when I seek You, the things will be added. It's not about the things anymore...my affection is set on You. Thank You for choosing me.

Medicine Music:
"I'll Just Say Yes"— Brian Courtney Wilson

Day 15: His Mark

Being confident of this, that he who began a good work in you will carry it on to completion until the day of Jesus Christ (Phil. 1:6).

The moment you begin to compare yourself to someone else, you lose. It doesn't matter if you're doing better or worse than the other person. When your view is on someone else's life, you prevent yourself from seeing God's true perspective of your own. You place unhealthy expectations on yourself and diminish who God has created you to be. Please do not forfeit your destiny by chasing someone else's. You will find yourself becoming a replica instead of an original.

"I press toward the mark for the prize of the high calling of God in Christ Jesus" (Philippians 3:14). Whose mark are you trying to hit? I've made the mistake of trying to hit other people's marks for my life. That can be detrimental. The moment you pursue somebody else's vision for your life, you lose time, energy and PASSION. Why the emphasis on passion? When you put time, energy, and resources into something that fails you, it will deplete you — deplete your joy, peace, and passion.

I challenge you to press toward His mark. The steps of a good man are ordered by the Lord. God has a plan for you, and He has put enough in you to accomplish it. If you pursue passionately His call for your life, you will find a fulfillment that you've never experienced. When you drop the weight of comparison, you will be light enough to fly right into purpose.

Pray This With Me:

Father, forgive me for seeing myself through the eyes of others. You've made me in Your image and likeness and have given me a measure of faith to carry out my assignment in the Kingdom. As I worship You, reveal to me Your image of me. I want to see myself as You see me and fulfill the purpose You created me to fulfill. I embrace the uniqueness of my design and determine to press toward You as I have never pressed before.

Medicine Music:
"Oh How I Need You"— All Sons & Daughters

Day 16: Today, We Sing

I will sing to the LORD all my life; I will sing praise to my God as long as I live (Ps. 104:33).

Today's devotional will be very short, simple, and to the point. I'm sure during this 21-day journey, some of you have said to yourself "This sure doesn't feel like a traditional worship devotional." Well, today is for you. Today we sing! It doesn't matter if you're on a worship team in a choir, or if you've never sung on any platform your entire life.

Today, we sing! In the shower, in your bedroom, in the car, in the hallways of your job. It doesn't matter where you are today; your job is to sing to the Lord.

Sing, oh barren! Rich, poor, broken, sick or healed — sing! If you've received good news or bad news, today, sing! He inhabits the praises of His people. Sing a song angels cannot sing—a song that has been written through the lenses of grace and mercy. Sing a song composed by a sinner who has been washed in the blood of the Lamb. Sing the song that only you know the lyrics to — lyrics that were birthed from countless blessings and victories given from our Savior. Sing! He wants to hear you. Yes, you. Sing! Sing! Sing!

Pray This With Me:

I choose to sing through my hurts, disappointments, and failures. You've given me a song that the angels can't sing...I'm redeemed. You see me as clean, whole, and healed, and I worship You for loving me more than I love myself. Let my song of worship be a sweet smelling savor to You.

Medicine Music:
"Fall In This Place"— Planet Shakers

Day 17: Excuses, Excuses, Excuses

For we know that our old self was crucified with him so that the body ruled by sin might be done away with, that we should no longer be slaves to sin (Rom. 6:6).

"This is just me." "This is who I am, so deal with it." "I was raised like this." I've been this way all my life." Have you ever heard anyone say any of these statements? Have you ever made one of them? They are all lazy excuses to avoid change. It's easy to make an excuse for why you behave the way do. There's no work involved in making an excuse. Yes, we are human, but the excuse, "I'm only human," can't work forever. At some point, you have to take responsibility for who you are and your actions. That, however, will never happen until you're honest. You might ask yourself, "Honest with whom?" Paul said, "When I was a child, I talked like a child, I thought like a child, I reasoned like a child. When I became a man, I put the ways of childhood behind me" (1 Cor 13:11). It's simply time to grow up and put in the work required to being a better person.

Excuses keep us from dealing with US. For a moment, let's try to take a deeper look at WHY we react or respond to certain situations or people the way we do. Is it a past hurt, disappointment, or rejection? Could it be fear? Let's get into His presence today and ask Him to show us. Some of us may already know the why. Let's give it to Him today. Let's lay down our excuses and take on the strength and courage to be vulnerable, to be honest, to be free from excuses.

PRAY THIS WITH ME:

I confess that I have been crucified with Christ. He now lives through me. I reject the old me and accept who Christ has made me to be. I put every excuse at the foot of the cross and apply the blood of Jesus to every nasty part of me. I am new! I am free! I am forgiven. Thank you, Jesus, for setting me free from myself.

Medicine Music:
"Moving Forward"—
Israel & New Breed

Day 18: You Are Enough

I praise you because I am fearfully and wonderfully made; your works are wonderful, I know that full well (Ps. 139:14).

You. Are. Enough. I'm sure you've been told otherwise by people or maybe even yourself, but today I need you to grasp this truth. You. Are. Enough. You are enough because you are not alone. Your being enough has very little to do with you and more to do with who's in you. Greater is he that is in me than he that's in the world." Not only is He in you, but He's for you, along with all of Heaven!. He also affirms you through His Word. His Word not only affirms you, but it validates you when people won't.

The enemy wants you to focus on past failures and the failures of those who are close to you. He wants to minimize the God that's for you and magnify the mountain in front of you. He's a great illusionist—always making things appear bigger than what they really are and making you THINK it's something that it's really not. You can't be moved by what you think. You have to be driven by what you KNOW. That's why praise is so important. It helps you keep God in proper perspective. "Oh magnify the Lord with me…" When you praise Him, you make Him bigger than your problems, insecurities, and fears.

Don't believe the lies. You are enough. You are not a failure, a mistake, inadequate or a loser. He calls you a conqueror, victorious—a champion! Rest in that TRUTH. God is for you and He's in you. You are enough because the God of more than enough lives in you!

PRAY THIS WITH ME:

Satan, I put you in your rightful place... under my feet. You have attempted to oppress me long enough with the guilt of my past. Jesus, I believe that when You hung on the tree at Calvary, You bore every curse so that I could be free. I denounce every curse that has attempted to attach itself to me. I'm healed, I'm free, I'm a conqueror. The curse is broken in my life.

Medicine Music:
"The Curse is Broken"— Todd Galberth

Day 19: For Good?

Trust in the LORD with all your heart and lean not on your own understanding; in all your ways submit to him, and he will make your paths straight (Prov. 3:5-6).

A friend called me to tell me about a decision that he and his spouse had made which had major, seemingly negative, long-term effects on their family. The friend is saved, loves the Lord, and is an avid worshipper. I listened as he and his spouse spoke about the details of the decision. They shared that they approached the situation with a solid plan in place; however, at the end of the day, the thing that they said they weren't going to do was the very thing they agreed to.

The friend asked, "How could I be so stupid?" "Why didn't I listen to the voice of the Lord," or better yet, "Why didn't I just stick to my plan?" I encouraged them and reminded them of Romans 8:28, "And we know that in all things God works for the good of those who love him, who have been called according to his purpose." The scripture doesn't say that God makes good decisions or smart moves work for our good. All means all. What does that mean to the believer? It means that we always win!

I want to encourage you. As humans, we make bad decisions, even with the best intentions. The good news is that loving God and being a true worshipper comes with benefits—He causes the worst decision or situation to work for you, not against you. I don't care how badly YOU messed up or how bad your current circumstance looks. God can't lie! He honors your heart that is turned toward Him and will work everything out in your favor! Worship reveals our frailty and His sovereignty. Yes, my brother and sister, good is going to come out of it. Worship through it.

PRAY THIS WITH ME:

Father, Your grace is sufficient. I believe that all things work together for my good because I love You. Thank You for continuing to help me trust Your plan for my life even when I seem to mess things up. Thank You for helping me forgive myself. Your strength is made perfect in my weakness. You're sovereign, omniscient,

83

omnipotent and ever present in my life. Receive my worship.

Medicine Music:
"Brokenness Aside"— All Sons & Daughters

Day 20: Happy with Me

For I know the plans I have for you," declares the LORD, "plans to prosper you and not to harm you, plans to give you hope and a future (Jer. 29:11).

One of the greatest gifts a father can give is affirmation. As a man thinketh in his heart, so is he. It's God's word that defines us. Understanding who you are can't start with who your parents are, how you were raised, or where you are from. It begins and ends with what the word of God says about you. If you're not careful, you will find yourself on an endless journey searching for your purpose and affirmation in other people.

If you purchase an item from a store and it breaks, you take it back to the place of purchase to get it fixed. The manufacturer made the item, so they know how to fix it. It doesn't make a lot of sense for you to find out how you're supposed to function from someone who didn't create you. If you're broken or confused, go back to the one who knows how to fix you and give you the answers you need.

If you're depending on people to affirm who you are, you're going to live on an emotional rollercoaster. People will adore you one day and destroy you the next. I'm talking about THE SAME PEOPLE! Just ask Jesus. It was "Hosannah" one week, then "crucify him" the next. He wasn't moved by the rejection

of men because he knew who He was."
This is my beloved son in whom I'm
well pleased." His father told Him who
He was. He didn't depend on the incon-
sistency of people for that.

God tells us very clearly who we are
in His Word. Rest in that. In the eyes
of man, you will continually be what
mankind conveniently wants you to
be. Know who you are, and live in that
peace and confidence.

PRAY THIS WITH ME:

*Father, you are the Potter; I am the clay.
You foreknew me and predestined me to
be in the image of Your Son, Jesus Christ.
I am honored to know that, regardless
of what others say, You see me as called,
justified and glorified. I thank you for
putting me back on the wheel every time
I lose focus on who you've called me to be.*

I realize that no human's opinion of me matters anymore. I love myself because You first loved me.

Medicine Music:
"Good Good Father"— Chris Tomlin

Day 21: Vertical

If my people, who are called by my name, will humble themselves and pray and seek my face and turn from their wicked ways, then I will hear from heaven, and I will forgive their sin and will heal their land (I Chron. 7:14).

In order to be a true worshipper, we have to have consistent, effective vertical communication with God. He waits and wants to hear from us. We actually want the same thing from each other. How do we keep the vertical connection solid? How do we maintain a posture of worship? How do we receive instructions for the next move? PRAYER! It's an absolute necessity.

There are different types of prayer in the church: prayers of supplication, intercession, faith, thanksgiving, and worship, to name a few. There is a type of prayer to appropriately address every facet of our lives. We must understand that the best way to REALLY get God's attention is to pray His Word. Before His Word fails, Heaven and Earth will pass away. God honors His Word. He responds to His Word. We have this assurance, but the clincher is…we must know His Word in order to pray His Word.

Make a conscious effort to read His Word daily, meditate on it, and quote it in prayer. The Bible is the roadmap of the worshipper. Let His Word flow through you. Your worship will increase as you continue to decrease.

Pray This With Me:

Father, I don't want anything to hinder my communication with you. Search my heart. Uproot any sin, unforgiveness, disbelief, ungratefulness or strife that will cause You not to hear me. Fill me with Your precious Holy Spirit so that I can pray Your Perfect Will. Let Your worship and Your Word flow through me like rivers of living water. I want to live a life that constantly brings glory to You. I believe that it shall be so.

Medicine Music:
"Our Father"— Bethel

CPSIA information can be obtained
at www.ICGtesting.com
Printed in the USA
FFHW021430071019
55373800-61145FF